Is Anger Always a Sin?

Crucial Questions booklets provide a quick introduction to definitive Christian truths. This expanding collection includes titles such as:

Who Is Jesus?

Can I Trust the Bible?

Does Prayer Change Things?

Can I Know God's Will?

How Should I Live in This World?

What Does It Mean to Be Born Again?

Can I Be Sure I'm Saved?

What Is Faith?

What Can I Do with My Guilt?

What Is the Trinity?

CQ

Is Anger Always a Sin?

R.C. SPROUL

Ligonier Ministries

Is Anger Always a Sin?

Published by Ligonier Ministries
421 Ligonier Court, Sanford, FL 32771
Ligonier.org

Printed in China
RR Donnelley
0001223
First edition

ISBN 978-1-64289-543-8 (Paperback)
ISBN 978-1-64289-544-5 (ePub)

Cover design: Ligonier Creative
Interior typeset: Katherine Lloyd, The DESK

Library of Congress Control Number: 2023933663

Contents

Chapter One

The Wrath of God

In the 1960s, when I was in graduate school in Europe, I was involved in a theological discussion about the developments in theology in the twentieth century. A great debate arose over a Latin phrase that had found its way into the confessions of historic Reformation theology: *placare ira Dei*. It means "to placate the wrath of God." The controversy had to do with how to understand the cross and specifically how to understand the atonement of Christ. Historically, Christian orthodoxy has always taught the following as one aspect of the atonement of Christ: Christ's sacrifice was designed to satisfy the demands of God's justice and to propitiate His wrath—that is, to assuage or to set aside His anger. The New Testament speaks of salvation in these terms, saying that Christ as our Savior has saved us from the wrath of God.

The wrath of God is a common theme in Scripture, and the Bible often speaks of Christ's atonement on the cross as satisfying God's wrath, so it may seem strange that anybody in the church would object to this phrase "to placate the wrath of God." Behind the controversy, however, was a growing trend in modern theology to deny that there is any wrath in God whatsoever. Many people don't like to think of the God of grace, love, and mercy as being given to anger, so in the liberal theology of the nineteenth century, there was a wholesale reaction against any notion of the wrath of God.

A truly biblical understanding of human anger must begin with a biblical understanding of God's anger. It may be surprising to hear that in the New Testament, the words *wrath* and *anger* occur more often with respect to God than words expressing God's love and mercy. If we want to deny the reality of the wrath of God, we're going to have to take some very large scissors to the pages of Scripture. Even a cursory reading of the Bible will reveal that the theology of sacred Scripture takes the wrath of God seriously.

In the first chapter of his letter to the Romans, beginning at verse 18, Paul makes this observation: "For the wrath of God is revealed from heaven against all ungodliness and unrighteousness of men, who by their unrighteousness suppress the truth."

Note Paul's introductory remark here: he speaks of the revelation of the wrath of God. The Greek word that is translated "wrath" is *orgē*. You may not be familiar with Greek at all, but that word might sound familiar nonetheless because of an English word that is derived from it: *orgy*.

An orgy was originally a cultic practice in the Greek and Roman pagan religions that involved uninhibited drunkenness and sexual expression. Such festivals honored the Roman god Bacchus or the Greek god Dionysius, the god of the vine or vineyard. These festivals involved excessive consumption of wine, the goal being to get drunk into a stupor in order to dull the thinking and senses and experience a spiritual kind of ecstasy.

The connection between an *orgy* and the Greek *orgē* is the idea of strong passion. When the Bible speaks of the wrath of God, it describes it not in terms of mild displeasure or a kind of divine irritation or annoyance but as an experience of strong feeling. Perhaps better than *wrath* would be the word *fury*. Paul is using strong language. He's speaking of a vehement anger that is revealed by God, who is moved to fury about certain things, and that fury is directed toward all unrighteousness and ungodliness of men. This is not an example of God's being angry over nothing or God's overreacting to a certain situation. Rather, it is His divine reaction to real wickedness, to actual evil in its destructive capacity.

When we talk about passions or emotions in connection with God, we must be careful not to project on God an equivalence or an identity between our modes of behavior or emotions and His. This is what we call an *anthropomorphic expression*—that is, God is being described in human terms.

Anger is something with which we are very familiar. It's not that we are supposed to come to the conclusion that God is a touchy deity who is given to temper tantrums. Rather, God's wrath expresses God's divine displeasure against evil. The Bible uses graphic terms and strong images to communicate this idea of God's sore displeasure. For instance, one of the most frightening statements about the wrath of God that we find anywhere is in Psalm 7: "God is a righteous judge, and a God who feels indignation every day. If a man does not repent, God will whet his sword; he has bent and readied his bow; he has prepared for him his deadly weapons, making his arrows fiery shafts" (vv. 11–13).

Perhaps the most famous sermon ever preached in America was Jonathan Edwards' "Sinners in the Hands of an Angry God." In college, a professor told my class that this sermon was the product of an unbalanced mind, that Edwards had this kind of fixation on and preoccupation with hellfire and damnation. He concluded that Edwards must have had a sadistic personality to have preached a sermon with such graphic images.

Edwards speaks of a spider, hanging by one thread of a web over open flames, and he says: "O sinner! You hang over the pit of hell suspended by one tiny thread; all the while the flames of divine wrath are burning and thrashing all around it, ready to singe it at any second and to drop you into the pit." Another image that he uses in that famous sermon is that of the bow of God. Edwards says, "God's bow is bent, and His arrow is aimed at your heart." You can imagine this bow's being pulled to its fullest extension, and you know that all it will take for the arrow aimed at your heart to be released is for God simply to open His fingers.

To call Edwards sadistic is to misunderstand the man completely. Edwards really believed in hell, he believed in the wrath of God, and most importantly, he believed that human beings are exposed to the reality of that wrath. Edwards cared about that. If he were sadistic, he would have told people just the opposite of what he did. He would have said: "Don't worry about it. God's not angry. Everything's OK. There is no hell." And he would have secretly enjoyed gleeful anticipation of these people's experiencing God's wrath in hell. Yet Edwards believed the Word of God and tried to awaken his people to the reality of it.

The psalmist says in Psalm 7 that first of all, God is a just Judge. Notice that the wrath of God is couched in terms of its relationship to God's justice. A perfectly holy judge of all the world who is incapable of being angry about evil could not possibly be good. God's anger is righteous indignation, and it is an appropriate response to the reality of injustice. It is injustice that angers God, and because He is just, because He is righteous, because He is holy, He has wrath.

The Scriptures repeatedly declare that God is slow to

anger. This is part of His forbearance and graciousness and long-suffering with our wickedness. Yet the Scriptures say something to us that we must not overlook. God is a just Judge, and God is angry with the wicked every day. If you are not a Christian, if you have not made peace with God, if you are still estranged from God, then you must understand that God is angry with you—and not only that, but He's angry with you every single day.

No one likes to have people mad at them. It's uncomfortable; it's intimidating; it's embarrassing. Yet even worse would be to have the God of heaven and earth angry with you every day. God's anger is real, and the ultimate source of it is God Himself, whose anger is always and everywhere just and justified.

We must take this seriously because the wrath of God is real. Yet His anger can be placated. There is a way of escaping His wrath, and that is found in the work of Christ. The cross of Christ was not simply a demonstration of Christ's meekness or of His righteousness or of His heroic self-giving. It was an act by which Jesus took on Himself the wrath that we deserve. He took that wrath for our sakes so that we do not have to ever worry about experiencing the wrath of God ourselves.

Chapter Two

The Anger of Christ

It's often been said that an army travels on its stomach. The troops must be well fed if they're going to be able to participate in battle. Yet the movement of armies has another dimension. Historically, songs have been of utmost importance; we see soldiers marching and shouting the cadence, and soon the cadence becomes a song.

In American lore, we have a history of battle songs or fight songs. Some of the lore that comes out of the Civil

War, for example, tells of episodes in which the Union army would be camped on one side of a river and the Confederate forces would be on the other side. On the night before the battle, the soldiers would be settled around their respective campfires, and they would sing their fight songs. As the Union soldiers gathered, they could hear the Confederates across the river as they sang "Dixie" or "When Johnny comes marching home again, Hurrah! Hurrah!"

What did the Union soldiers sing as their rallying fight song? It became ingrained in the music tradition of the whole nation after the war: the "Battle Hymn of the Republic." Think of the words of that song. It's an intensely religious and theologically loaded text: "Mine eyes have seen the glory of the coming of the Lord; He is trampling out the vintage where the grapes of wrath are stored; He hath loosed the fateful lightning of His terrible swift sword: His truth is marching on."

These words are based on concepts recorded in Scripture. The chief text that served as the inspiration is found in Revelation 14. The scene just before in John's vision was of the bowls of God's wrath being poured out from heaven. In verses 14–20, we read:

Then I looked, and behold, a white cloud, and seated on the cloud one like a son of man, with a golden crown on his head, and a sharp sickle in his hand. And another angel came out of the temple, calling with a loud voice to him who sat on the cloud, "Put in your sickle, and reap, for the hour to reap has come, for the harvest of the earth is fully ripe." So he who sat on the cloud swung his sickle across the earth, and the earth was reaped.

Then another angel came out of the temple in heaven, and he too had a sharp sickle. And another angel came out from the altar, the angel who has authority over the fire, and he called with a loud voice to the one who had the sharp sickle, "Put in your sickle and gather the clusters from the vine of the earth, for its grapes are ripe." So the angel swung his sickle across the earth and gathered the grape harvest of the earth and threw it into the great winepress of the wrath of God. And the winepress was trodden outside the city, and blood flowed from the winepress, as high as a horse's bridle, for 1,600 stadia.

The song says, "He is trampling out the vintage where the grapes of wrath are stored; He hath loosed the fateful lightning of His terrible swift sword." These words capture the biblical image of the last judgment, when Christ comes to manifest the wrath of God. We don't normally think of Jesus in these terms, and yet the Scriptures point to that coming day, the day of the Lord, the day of darkness with no light in it, as a time of reaping, a time of division, a time of judgment when God will apply the sickle to the plants and cut down all those who are in resistance against Christ.

Throughout the Bible, we are given other images of that final manifestation of the anger of God. Think of Psalm 2, which describes a conspiracy of the nations. The kings of the earth take counsel together and set themselves against the Lord and against His Anointed, saying, "Let us burst their bonds apart and cast away their cords from us" (v. 3). All the leaders and powers of the world gather in a summit meeting to join forces against the reign of God and against the reign of His Messiah—and the response from heaven is that the Lord laughs. God holds them in derision. Then the psalm goes on to say that God's anger is kindled in a moment, and at the end is this admonition: "Kiss the Son, lest he be angry, and you perish in the way" (v. 12).

Psalm 2 brings together not only the wrath of God the Father but also a sober warning and admonition regarding the anger of the Son of God. We are told in Scripture that at Christ's coming, every knee will bow before Him. When we look closely at the imagery used in the description of that universal bowing of the knee before Christ when He comes in the consummation of His kingdom, we see that the knees are bowed for different reasons. Those who love Him and rejoice in His appearance willingly, gratefully, and quickly bow their knees before Him in humble adoration and affection, but those who are the enemies of Christ will also bow down. Why will they bow? Because their knees will be broken with the rod of His iron. Everyone will bow—some willingly in reverent worship, others unwillingly because their knees have been broken and smashed by the anger of God.

What do the Scriptures teach us about Christ? The Bible tells us that Christ came to reveal the Father. He is the express image of the Father, the brightness of His glory, and He most perfectly reveals to us the character of God.

If anger or wrath were inherently evil, intrinsically bad or wicked, then it would be a defect in the character of God for Him to be angry, and it would be a defect in

Jesus' nature for Him to ever become angry. Part of the message of the New Testament about Christ is the declaration of His sinlessness. Christ fulfills the role of the Lamb without blemish. He cannot qualify as the One who offers a perfect sacrifice for His people if any sin is found in Him. He cannot qualify as the grounds of our justification by His perfect obedience and by His merit if He commits even a single sin. If Jesus commits one sin, He can't do anything to atone for His one sin, let alone to atone for our sins. So one of the biblical requirements for the Messiah to fulfill His office of saving His people is absolute sinlessness.

There are occasions in the New Testament when Jesus becomes angry and exhibits that anger. We are also told, as we've already seen, that Scripture predicts an even greater manifestation of His anger in the future. These episodes are expressions not of wickedness but of virtue. There is such a thing as righteous indignation.

A specific example in the New Testament that most clearly demonstrates the anger of Christ is His clearing the temple. We know how He responded to the Pharisees when He spoke to them in the sharpest tones, strongly rebuking them by calling them serpents, calling them children of hell, using strong language in His denunciation. Yet His anger was even more strongly kindled when He came to Jerusalem and entered the temple. There, He saw the money-changers. Who were the money-changers, and what were they doing in the temple?

Every Israelite had the spiritual obligation to come to the temple at appointed times to offer sacrifices, and the Jews of the Diaspora and the Jews from the outer districts made pilgrimages to Jerusalem regularly. The journey was difficult and often very long. When people made these trips, they would not take their goats or sheep from their herds where they lived and drive those animals all the way to Jerusalem for sacrifice. That would have been too expensive. Instead, the temple authorities kept animals close by. Shepherds took care of them and carefully ensured that they were without blemish, and then the animals were sold to the pilgrims who needed them for sacrifice. In fact, it's probable that the shepherds who were out at night in Bethlehem when Jesus was born were tending the temple sheep.

Because buying sheep was necessary for the people to keep the law, the temple authorities kept raising the prices and taking advantage of those who had to purchase them.

Not only that, but the scam got worse when the money-changers entered the picture. The different currency from outside Jerusalem, and outside the country at times, was not accepted by those who were selling the animals for temple use. Therefore, they positioned money-changers right in the temple, and those money-changers charged exorbitant exchange rates.

Perhaps you've traveled abroad before the widespread use of debit and credit cards. If so, you know what it's like to exchange your currency for that of the country you're visiting. When you turn in your dollars to get pesos or euros or yen, the money-changer takes his cut during the process, so you always lose something when you trade that money. That's what was going on in the temple.

Jesus came to the temple for worship, and He saw that the temple had become a huge trading mall with money being exchanged at usurious rates and that people were being exploited for commercial reasons at the very point where they were trying to fulfill their spiritual duty. What did Jesus do? Did He say, "I'd like to make a suggestion about ways to improve the temple practices here"? Or did He walk over to the chief priests and say: "I think maybe you've overlooked something here. This practice that you have going on here in the temple is not quite consistent with what My Father had in mind for worship"?

No, that was not His reaction. The Bible says something extraordinary about Jesus. It tells us that He actually fashioned a whip and went into the temple in a furious rage, kicking over the tables and scattering the money. He tore down the booths and drove the money-changers out of the temple. He said, "Don't you know that My Father's house is to be a house of prayer, and you've turned it into a den of thieves, into a house of merchandise?"

If any one incident really provoked the wrath of the Sadducees and of the priests against Christ and caused them to plot against His life, it was His clearing the temple. Jesus was no longer just preaching; now He was meddling. Jesus was upsetting their economy at this point, and He was taking money out of their pockets. Jesus was furious that people were taking the truths of God and using them for selfish gain that exploited oppressed people. That was not an example of an ill-tempered Christ; it was an example of the *holy* Christ whose wrath was kindled by that which was not holy. This was real righteous indignation.

As we seek to understand human wrath, we must discern when it is righteous and when it is unrighteous. Our anger can go both ways. Our anger can be justifiable, or it can be the occasion of destruction, violence, bitterness, and all kinds of evil. In Christ, there was anger, but there was never a misuse of anger. That cannot be said for us.

Chapter Three

Be Angry but Don't Sin

The Christian life, in many ways, is a life of responding to divine imperatives. An imperative expresses an obligation. It is a way of saying what we must do. All languages have some way of expressing necessity by way of the imperative. That was also true, of course, in the Greek language in which the New Testament was written.

There are many imperatives in the New Testament, but one of them may strike us as somewhat strange. In Ephesians 4:25–27, Paul writes: "Therefore, having put away falsehood, let each one of you speak the truth with his neighbor, for we are members of one another. Be angry and do not sin; do not let the sun go down on your anger, and give no opportunity to the devil."

The main thrust of this passage is a warning about a misuse of anger. Notice, however, the strange way that Paul introduces the subject. He begins with an imperative: "Be angry." He will go on to qualify that statement, but here we actually get an exhortation to do something. The Word of God tells us, with the imperative form, to be angry. Isn't that strange? Doesn't that seem utterly inconsistent with everything else that we learn in Scripture about norms for human behavior? We don't want to be known as angry people, do we? Yet the Bible says, "Be angry."

The general principles of Christian behavior call us to be imitators of Christ, who Himself imitated God. Christian virtue is a matter of being an imitator of someone else who reveals the standard of perfect righteousness to us. The logic goes as follows: There are times when God is angry and there are times when Christ is angry; therefore, there are times when we should be angry.

The anger of God and the anger of Christ are, of course, always righteous. This imperative to "be angry" is not a license for the expression of any kind or force of anger; rather, the anger that we are called to exhibit must also be imitative. It must be like the anger of God in the sense that it must be righteous and not just selfish and explosive.

There are times when it is appropriate and even required that we be angry. It is not that it's a sinful occasion every time that we're angry. Some things that go on in the world, in schools, in the government, and in the church ought to make us angry. When the truth of God is maligned and distorted, we should be angry about that. When human beings are violated, we should be angry about that. When we're not angry about it, it reveals a profound indifference to sacred things. The key, however, is to have our responses mirror the responses of Christ. We should be angry at the things that Christ is angry about and not angry at the things that He's not angry about.

One of the noteworthy things about Jesus was the different ways that He related to different people. There were times that He came into contact with sinners who were involved in very serious sin, and He related to them in a profoundly gentle, sensitive, caring, forgiving way. One such occasion is found in John 8. A woman caught in adultery was dragged to the feet of Jesus, and the man involved wasn't brought to Jesus. The Pharisees used this as an occasion to trap Jesus. And they weren't concerned about this woman's morality. They were concerned about utterly destroying her. They didn't care about her forgiveness or her rehabilitation.

This was an occasion when Jesus was very calm. He bent down to write on the ground, and then He said, "Let him who is without sin among you be the first to throw a stone at her" (John 8:7). One by one, the accusers went away, and Jesus was left alone with the woman. What do the Scriptures say next? "Then He poured out His wrath on her and said: 'What's the matter with you, you wicked woman, being involved in this adulterous relationship? I should have had them stone you to death.'" Jesus could have done that and would have been justified in doing so, but that's not what He did. He said: "Woman, where are they? Has no one condemned you?" (v. 10). She looked around, and she said to Him, "No one, Lord." Then Jesus declared, "Neither do I condemn you; go, and from now on sin no more" (v. 11). Notice that He did rebuke her. He didn't say, "Go and keep on sinning, and it doesn't matter if you continue this kind of practice." Yet we must notice the calm spirit that Jesus exhibited and how tender He was with her. She was guilty, but He understood that she realized that she was guilty, and He knew that her spirit was humble, contrite, and broken. There was no need for Jesus to pour out His anger on her.

Instead, He was angry with those who were the leaders. When Jesus dealt with the ordained clergy of His day, with the leaders of the community, with those in the seats of power and of authority, He gave no quarter. He didn't put up with hypocrisy or injustice from them. He showed them His wrath. Yet with the broken and downtrodden, He was tender.

Leo Durocher was a Major League Baseball manager and the author of *Nice Guys Finish Last*. He was once asked about his secret to managing baseball players. He replied, "My secret is that I treat every person on my team exactly the same way." I thought, "That's a lousy way to coach." If he meant that everybody has to play by the same rules and everybody has the same requirements, OK. Some people need to be treated tenderly, however, and other people need to be treated with greater strength. If we're going to relate to all different kinds of people, it takes great wisdom to know when to be tender and when to be strong.

Jesus mastered that balance. He always seemed to save His anger for those who really should have known better and who were in positions of power and authority. So there is a place and a time and a way for Christians to reflect the anger of Christ in a righteous way. Yet if there's any emotion that is laced with danger and can be the occasion for the destruction of other people and of our own souls, if not guarded and tempered by the truth of God, it is anger.

Paul states, "Be angry." He doesn't go on to say after that, "I want you to be as angry as you can be all the time." Rather, he says, "Be angry and do not sin," because he understands that the emotion of anger is a powerful impetus for sin. When we become angry, we can overreact. We can become violent. We can become hateful. We can become bitter. We must be careful about where our anger takes us.

At the opposite extreme, some Christians believe that it's a sin to grieve, that if their spouse or their child dies, they're supposed to act like stoics and smile all the way through the funeral. Yet the Scriptures tell us that Jesus was a man of sorrows, acquainted with grief. He wept at the death of His friend Lazarus.

Grief is a legitimate human emotion. Special blessings are promised to those who mourn. Those emotions are fine, just as the emotion of anger is fine. But emotions can be dangerous because if we do not find our comfort in

God, they can easily slip into self-pity or bitterness. The author of Hebrews warns about allowing a root of bitterness to spring up in the soul, by which our lives are spoiled (Heb. 12:15). Do you see what a short journey it is from grief to self-pity, from grief to bitterness, from anger to bitterness? There are a lot of angry people in this world whose anger has eaten away their souls. Their anger has been pent up inside for so long that it has slowly but surely eroded their very character. As a result, they come across as angry, hostile people who have become bitter people.

So Paul admonishes us to be angry and not to sin because he understands that anger can be, and often is, the occasion for sin. What's his remedy? "Be angry and do not sin; do not let the sun go down on your anger." What does he mean by that? You can be as mad as you want in the daytime, but as soon as the sun sets, you can't be mad at anything that happens? The sunset is not the point. This was a proverbial expression among the Jews: "Don't let the sun set on your wrath." What is meant by that? Don't harbor it. Don't nurture it. Don't hold on to it; instead, let it dissipate, let it go away. This is often hard for us, especially in our relationships with the people we are closest to. We get angry, and then we sin and we harbor grudges. We begin to feed and to nurture animosity and a lust for revenge and an attempt to get even in order to hurt the person who has hurt us.

Paul instructs, "Be angry and do not sin; do not let the sun go down on your anger, and give no opportunity to the devil." According to the proverbial saying, idle hands are the devil's workshop. I would say, no, it's unresolved anger that is the workshop of Satan. If he can take an otherwise healthy person and distort and twist his anger and make it bitterness, he can destroy that soul along with a lot of other people along the way.

Later in this same passage, Paul exhorts: "And do not grieve the Holy Spirit of God, by whom you were sealed for the day of redemption. Let all bitterness and wrath and anger and clamor and slander be put away from you, along with all malice. Be kind to one another, tenderhearted, forgiving one another, as God in Christ forgave you" (Eph. 4:30–32). The keyword in that passage is *malice*. That's the danger lurking in the shadows of anger: that anger can make us malicious people. In the criminal justice system, *malice aforethought* refers to something that is done with angry intention, with purpose to harm other people. That is a fruit of unresolved anger.

We are allowed to be angry. Indeed, according to the Word of God, we are required to be angry about certain things. That anger, however, must always be brought *coram Deo*, before the face of God, and judged by the standard of His righteousness and of His anger.

Chapter Four

When Anger Destroys

Jacob, whose name was changed to Israel, is well known for his sons, who became the twelve tribes of Israel. He was also blessed with daughters, one of whom was named Dinah. She was a key figure in an incident of great pain and scandal in Old Testament history. We read of this account in the book of Genesis:

> Now Dinah the daughter of Leah, whom she had borne to Jacob, went out to see the women of the

> land. And when Shechem the son of Hamor the Hivite, the prince of the land, saw her, he seized her and lay with her and humiliated her. And his soul was drawn to Dinah the daughter of Jacob. He loved the young woman and spoke tenderly to her. So Shechem spoke to his father Hamor, saying, "Get me this girl for my wife."
>
> Now Jacob heard that he had defiled his daughter Dinah. But his sons were with his livestock in the field, so Jacob held his peace until they came. (Gen. 34:1–5)

A man named Shechem becomes infatuated with Dinah and violates her. This is a dreadful crime against this girl and against her family. Jacob hears about it, and he is very upset, but he holds his peace until he can have a complete hearing on the matter and discuss it with his sons.

When his sons return, they are incensed: "The sons of Jacob had come in from the field as soon as they heard of it, and the men were indignant and very angry, because he had done an outrageous thing in Israel by lying with Jacob's daughter, for such a thing must not be done" (v. 7). The brothers of Dinah have reason to be angry. The crime against their sister, as the Scriptures say, is something that ought not to have been done, and so the brothers are justifiably angry.

Jacob then deals with the young man and his father, seeking peace and reconciliation. The request is made for the hand of Dinah, and Jacob agrees to it, but only on certain conditions. He says, "I can't allow my daughter to marry pagans, uncircumcised Gentiles." Shechem and his family agree to be circumcised, along with all their men, so that Shechem can marry Dinah and make some kind of compensation for this crime against her. Apparently all this satisfies Jacob, but it doesn't satisfy the brothers. Now see what happens toward the end of the story:

> On the third day, when they were sore, two of the sons of Jacob, Simeon and Levi, Dinah's brothers, took their swords and came against the city while it felt secure and killed all the males. They killed Hamor and his son Shechem with the sword and took Dinah out of Shechem's house and went away. The sons of Jacob came upon the slain and plundered the city, because they had defiled their sister. They took their flocks and their herds, their

> donkeys, and whatever was in the city and in the field. All their wealth, all their little ones and their wives, all that was in the houses, they captured and plundered. (vv. 25–29)

Jacob finds out what has happened and says to his sons: "You have brought trouble on me by making me stink to the inhabitants of the land, the Canaanites and the Perizzites. My numbers are few, and if they gather themselves against me and attack me, I shall be destroyed, both I and my household." The sons respond, "Should he treat our sister like a prostitute?" (vv. 30–31). They're saying: "What's the matter with you, Father? Are you going to let these people get away with this crime? All we did was avenge our sister."

"Is that all?" Jacob says. "You killed a man, and you killed his father. You killed every male in the city who had come under my protection, trusting my promise of peace. And not only did you rise up and kill them, but you took their children captive. You plundered their villages. You took all their possessions. You went out on a vendetta. You didn't get revenge. You didn't get even. You became bloodthirsty."

How many times has this happened in human history, when one incident escalates to something with enormous consequences? Why did it happen? Because Levi and his brother were angry. Their anger was justifiable, but in their anger they sinned. Let's look at the consequences of their actions.

At the end of the book of Genesis is the record of Jacob's deathbed address to his sons, when he gives his patriarchal blessing and divides up his inheritance among them. We read: "Then Jacob called his sons and said, 'Gather yourselves together, that I may tell you what shall happen to you in days to come. Assemble and listen, O sons of Jacob, listen to Israel your father. Reuben, you are my firstborn, my might, and the firstfruits of my strength, preeminent in dignity and preeminent in power. Unstable as water, you shall not have preeminence, because you went up to your father's bed; then you defiled it—he went up to my couch!'" (Gen. 49:1–4).

According to the custom of the time, the firstborn was to receive the largest share of the inheritance. Part of the inheritance of Jacob was the promise of God of a coming kingdom. Reuben as the firstborn should have received this promise. Yet in the New Testament, Jesus is never called "the Lion of Reuben." No, Judah received the promise of the kingdom instead. Jesus the Messiah comes from the tribe of Judah, not from the tribe of Reuben. Reuben, because of his incestuous act, was cut out of the inheritance.

This suggests that the next person in line to receive the inheritance would be the next eldest. So Jacob goes right down the list; the next eldest is Simeon, followed by Levi. Jacob continues in verses 5–6: "Simeon and Levi are brothers; weapons of violence are their swords. Let my soul come not into their council." In other words, Jacob wishes to keep them away from him. He doesn't want to be a part of their schemes. "O my glory, be not joined to their company" (v. 6). What do you suppose Jacob's thinking about here? Perhaps he's thinking back to his lament that he had become a reproach to the nations because of the cruelty of his sons, that his reputation had been spoiled, that his word had been violated, and that he had been brought into dishonor because of his sons' actions.

Notice what he goes on to state: "For in their anger they killed men, and in their willfulness they hamstrung oxen. Cursed be their anger, for it is fierce, and their wrath, for it is cruel! I will divide them in Jacob and scatter them in

Israel" (vv. 6–7). Judah's elder brothers are passed over, two of them as a direct result of a sinful expression of anger.

Is this an isolated incident in the Old Testament, when people in their anger do things that are so destructive, so violent, and so cruel that they themselves miss the kingdom? Consider the wrath of Saul, the first king of Israel, who received the kingdom but had it taken away because of his irrational tantrums and tirades of violence.

David almost lost the kingdom for the same reason. At one time in David's life, he was a renegade outlaw in the wilderness—furious, angry, bitter, and violent—and it was during this period that the incident took place with Nabal and Abigail. In 1 Samuel 25, we read of something that happened immediately after the death of Samuel: "And there was a man in Maon whose business was in Carmel. The man was very rich; he had three thousand sheep and a thousand goats. He was shearing his sheep in Carmel. Now the name of the man was Nabal, and the name of his wife Abigail. The woman was discerning and beautiful, but the man was harsh and badly behaved; he was a Calebite" (vv. 2–3).

David heard reports that this very wealthy man by the name of Nabal had come to the time in the season for the shearing of sheep, which is a very laborious and expensive enterprise. David's men were short on provisions, and David had been very careful to honor the possessions of Nabal. Outlaws will typically pillage the land, take their provisions by force from the local farmers, and so on. David's men had not done that. David's men had been very careful not only not to violate the property of Nabal but actually to help Nabal's men in taking care of the flocks.

David sent a message to Nabal, asking for some small provisions and volunteers to help him with this shearing season. Nabal responded in this way: "And Nabal answered David's servants, 'Who is David? Who is the son of Jesse? There are many servants these days who are breaking away from their masters. Shall I take my bread and my water and my meat that I have killed for my shearers and give it to men who come from I do not know where?' So David's young men turned away and came back and told him all this" (vv. 10–12).

This was taking place in a land where probably the most famous person in all the country was David. This was the man who had killed Goliath. Nabal certainly knew who David was. He not only refused David's humble request but insulted him as well. David's servants came back and told this to David.

David's reaction is found in verse 13: "And David said

to his men, 'Every man strap on his sword!' And every man of them strapped on his sword. David also strapped on his sword. And about four hundred men went up after David, while two hundred remained with the baggage." David was angry, and he set out to go after Nabal. He was thinking: "Who does this fellow think he is? I haven't harmed him. I've protected him. I've been kind to him. And this is the thanks I get? I've had it. I'm taking my soldiers, and we're going to take this guy out."

The story goes on:

> One of the young men told Abigail, Nabal's wife, "Behold, David sent messengers out of the wilderness to greet our master, and he railed at them. Yet the men were very good to us, and we suffered no harm, and we did not miss anything when we were in the fields, as long as we went with them. They were a wall to us both by night and by day, all the while we were with them keeping the sheep. Now therefore know this and consider what you should do, for harm is determined against our master and against all his house, and he is such a worthless man that one cannot speak to him." (vv. 14–17)

Abigail hurried up, took two hundred loaves of bread, two skins of wine, five sheep, roasted grain, clusters of raisins, and two hundred cakes and loaded them on donkeys. She went to meet David while Nabal was hiding back at the ranch. Abigail knew that David was coming with an army against their homestead in furious revenge. She made a peace offering, bringing all that David had requested and much more. Abigail saw David approaching, got off her donkey, and fell to the ground before David and apologized for her husband, begging for David's mercy.

What did David do? Did he say, "This has nothing to do with you; I want your husband"? No. Here's David's response: "Blessed be the LORD, the God of Israel, who sent you this day to meet me! Blessed be your discretion, and blessed be you, who have kept me this day from bloodguilt and from working salvation with my own hand!" (vv. 32–33). That's the difference between David and Levi and Simeon. The brothers could not be stopped from their fury until they had killed all the people associated with the affront against their sister.

David was about to do exactly the same thing until Abigail stopped him and pleaded with him. Suddenly, the sun went down on David's wrath and he said: "Thank you.

In my anger, in my fury, in my wrath, I was about to use my sword and spill blood and bring dishonor to everyone involved." That night, God judged Nabal and took his life. Then Abigail, who had provided wise and peaceful counsel, became the wife of David.

On the one hand, the sons of Jacob violated their father, violated their people, and violated God; it cost them the kingdom of God. David almost did the same thing but was prevented by the wisdom and counsel of a woman who was wiser than David. These stories illustrate what the Bible says about anger: "Be angry and do not sin; do not let the sun go down on your anger" (Eph. 4:26). Fortunately, David stopped short of violating God at this point, so that the Messiah was not called "the Son of Levi" or "the Son of Reuben" or "the Son of Simeon," but was called "the Son of David."

Chapter Five

Dealing with Anger

Having seen that there is a legitimate place for anger but how anger can have disastrous consequences, we must look at anger's root causes and explore some practical suggestions for how we as Christians can learn how to manage anger and exercise the Spirit's fruit of self-control.

A friend once said that he looks at every person he meets as a large open field, and he assumes that in that field land mines are buried beneath the surface. As he continued with this analogy, he said that some people have only a couple of minor mines buried in their field, and you can traverse the field back and forth and possibly never step on one. Other people's personalities seem to be like a field that is wall-to-wall land mines, and wherever you step, you get an explosive reaction.

We all have mines buried somewhere in our personalities. Not everyone gets irritated or angered by the same things. Some of us can remain very calm when the airplane is late, while other people begin to fret and fume and to get angrier and angrier. Tolerance levels differ from person to person, and there are personal reasons why things make us angry.

Socrates was convinced that there is a correlation between right behavior and right understanding. For example, if you wanted to develop the character trait of courage, the way to do it was to come to an intellectual understanding of what courage actually is. The problem with Socrates is that he tended to reduce all these behavioral patterns simply to the cognitive level, to the level of knowledge, and he tended to minimize or overlook entirely the emotional dimension that is so vital to an understanding of these behavioral patterns. Yet he was right in his recognition that there is a real correlation between our understanding and our behavior.

Socrates was really echoing something that is found throughout the Scriptures—namely, that the way to the heart is through the understanding, through the mind. If we're having difficulty controlling our emotions and our passions, it helps us at a very practical level to try to understand the nature of anger—what causes anger, what it looks like, how to control it, what different types of anger there are—and then to see whether we can relate to this in terms of our own patterns of behavior.

The first principle to consider is the most important in trying to understand anger. Almost all (if not all) anger is rooted and grounded in some kind of pain. Anger doesn't occur in a vacuum. Think about what makes you angry. If somebody walked up to you and slapped you across the face, chances are that it would annoy you. And it might make you furious. The initial response is to the physical pain that you have just experienced.

Yet physical pain is not the only kind of pain. If someone steals your property, that might make you angry because you've experienced a kind of personal loss. Somebody else may make you angry by insulting you or criticizing you. Out of that pain then comes the anger.

What happens if someone hurts us and our pain goes

to anger and we express that anger? Anger usually elicits a response of anger in return. In our anger, we hurt others. Then the other person responds by being angry with us, and that response of anger hurts us. On and on it goes. It can actually end in any number of violent expressions. If that cycle can be stopped early, so much of the pain and the further destruction can be averted.

To stop the cycle earlier, we need to understand the relationship between anger and pain. When someone is angry with us, we must look past the anger and try to find the pain. If we can hear and understand the pain behind the anger, we're going to be in a much better position to alleviate the pain rather than multiply it.

The pain that we experience can be of different sorts. For instance, there is situational anger, in which anger is caused by one situation but is expressed in a separate context. For instance, a man might have a stressful day at work and come home and unload on his wife and children. He is not able to express his anger at work; he has to keep it bottled up. His anger then grows and multiplies until he finally lets it out.

We've all experienced becoming the target of somebody's misplaced anger. We didn't do anything to cause the pain, but the situation was such that the person was wounded and hurt, and he then lashed out at the first human being he came across. We need to be able to recognize situational anger of this type and to see it, in many cases, as misdirected anger. We are surely all guilty of misdirected anger as well, when we direct our anger at an innocent person because he happens to be the closest one there and we're frustrated.

There is no instant cure for this, but we can gain progress if we understand what is going on. It may help to ask ourselves some basic human questions: What tends to make you mad? Where are your areas of intolerance? What behavioral characteristics of people really annoy you? After you identify the things that typically make you mad, then ask yourself the next question: Why? Why do these things make you mad?

Some things can become very complex and complicated. One of the things that I really can't stand is cowardliness, people who cave under pressure and flee in the midst of pressing circumstances. The movie *Patton* has a scene in which General Patton slaps a cowardly soldier, and he is furious. That slapping incident became an international incident. It's interesting how people in the theater who watched *Patton* had totally different reactions to it. Some people were furious at Patton because the thing they couldn't stand was a bully beating up on a weak person. Seeing a general come and slap the face of a subordinate, insulting his dignity, was just intolerable to many people in the theater. My own sympathies were with Patton. I just couldn't stand to see this coward who had exposed his comrades to danger through his cowardice.

I asked myself, "Why do I react like that?" I think I know. I have fears of my own, and in my heart dwells the inclination to be a coward. I don't like to be afraid, and I know that cowardice is contagious just as courage is contagious. I want to be around people who are manifesting courage because they inspire me and keep me from surrendering to my own human weakness. I want to distance myself from cowardly people because I'm afraid I'll become one of them. Other people have different psychological inclinations toward different life situations. We must seek to understand our own anger because until we do, we will not be able to control it.

We must also ask ourselves how we handle anger. As Christians, we are called not to respond in anger but to absorb it. We're supposed to have a charity that covers a multitude of sins. This gets harder and harder the more someone sins against us or offends us or hurts us. Rather than exploding in a release of pent-up frustration, we must strive to handle the offenses of others in a Christlike way, in a way that is not violent or vituperative. When we do this by the power of the Holy Spirit, we mirror the righteousness and patience of God.

About the Author

Dr. R.C. Sproul was founder of Ligonier Ministries, first minister of preaching and teaching at Saint Andrew's Chapel in Sanford, Fla., first president of Reformation Bible College, and executive editor of *Tabletalk* magazine. His radio program, *Renewing Your Mind*, is still broadcast daily on hundreds of radio stations around the world and can also be heard online. He was author of more than one hundred books, including *The Holiness of God*, *Chosen by God*, and *Everyone's a Theologian*. He was recognized throughout the world for his articulate defense of the inerrancy of Scripture and the need for God's people to stand with conviction upon His Word.

Your Questions. Trustworthy Answers.

Have you ever had questions about a passage in the Bible but you didn't know where to go for answers? Has a theological issue sent you searching far and wide for answers you can trust? *Ask Ligonier* is a podcast that allows listeners like you to submit questions about the Bible, theology, the Christian life, and more to trustworthy Bible teachers. Every Thursday, Nathan W. Bingham submits your questions to one of Ligonier Ministries' Teaching Fellows or a special guest. Each teacher draws from years of careful study to provide knowledgeable, accessible answers you can trust.

JUST SEARCH FOR "**LIGONIER MINISTRIES**" IN YOUR FAVORITE PODCAST APP.